BABY ANIMALS

BABY SEA LIONS

Martha E. H. Rustad

a Capstone company — publishers for children

Raintree is an imprint of Capstone Global Library Limited, a company incorporated in England and Wales having its registered office at 264 Banbury Road, Oxford, OX2 7DY – Registered company number: 6695582

www.raintree.co.uk
myorders@raintree.co.uk

Hardback edition © Capstone Global Library Limited 2022
Paperback edition © Capstone Global Library Limited 2023
The moral rights of the proprietor have been asserted.

All rights reserved. No part of this publication may be reproduced in any form or by any means (including photocopying or storing it in any medium by electronic means and whether or not transiently or incidentally to some other use of this publication) without the written permission of the copyright owner, except in accordance with the provisions of the Copyright, Designs and Patents Act 1988 or under the terms of a licence issued by the Copyright Licensing Agency, 5th Floor, Shackleton House, 4 Battle Bridge Lane, London SE1 2HX (www.cla.co.uk). Applications for the copyright owner's written permission should be addressed to the publisher.

Edited by Alison Deering
Designed by Jennifer Bergstrom
Original illustrations © Capstone Global Library Limited 2022
Picture research by Tracy Cummins
Production by Tori Abraham
Originated by Capstone Global Library Ltd

978 1 3982 2405 6 (hardback)
978 1 3982 2406 3 (paperback)

British Library Cataloguing in Publication Data
A full catalogue record for this book is available from the British Library.

Acknowledgements
We would like to thank the following for permission to reproduce photographs: BluePlanetArchive.com: Mark Conlin, 13; Shutterstock: Andrea Izzotti, 12, Anna Om, 16, Blue Ice, 6, Daniel Avram, 19, Eric Isselee, back cover, Foto 4440, cover, 7, 9, imageBROKER.com, 14, kongsak sumano, 5, Leonardo Gonzalez, 11, Monkey Business Images, 20, NATTHAWAT PHROMTHAISONG, 21, Sydni Josowitz, 17, wildestanimal, 15.

Every effort has been made to contact copyright holders of material reproduced in this book. Any omissions will be rectified in subsequent printings if notice is given to the publisher.

All the internet addresses (URLs) given in this book were valid at the time of going to press. However, due to the dynamic nature of the internet, some addresses may have changed, or sites may have changed or ceased to exist since publication. While the author and publisher regret any inconvenience this may cause readers, no responsibility for any such changes can be accepted by either the author or the publisher.

Printed and bound in India

Contents

A newborn pup 4

Learning and growing 10

All grown up 18

Sea lions and fish 20

    Glossary 22

    Find out more 23

    Index 24

Words in **bold** are in the glossary.

A NEWBORN PUP

A new baby is here! It is a sea lion **pup**. The pup grew inside its mother for about a year. Now it stays close to her. It drinks milk from its mother's body.

Sea lions are sea animals. They come on land to have babies. Family groups gather on beaches or on ice. A group is made up of one male and many females.

The mother stays close to her baby for several days. She leaves when it's time to eat. She must find food in the sea.

Pups gather in groups while their mothers are hunting. They walk on their **flippers**. They play and make noises.

When a mother comes back, she calls for her baby. The pup hears her. It makes its own sound. The mother and pup know each other's noises.

A seal pup weighs about 6 to 9 kilograms (13 to 20 pounds) at birth. It is born with baby fur. The fur keeps it warm until it grows **blubber**. Blubber is a layer of fat.

Pups shed their baby fur after a few months. Adult fur grows in. Adult males have **manes** of thick fur, just like lions. That is how sea lions got their name.

LEARNING AND GROWING

Pups have to learn a lot in their first year. They learn by copying adults. Mothers teach their babies to swim. They start in shallow water. Then they learn to swim in deep water.

Sea lions can dive deep underwater. Some stay under as long as 30 minutes. They close their **nostrils**. They use their flippers to swim.

11

Sea lions can swim very fast. Their top speed is 40 kilometres (25 miles) per hour. Swimming fast helps them catch **prey**.

Sea lions also swim fast to get away from **predators**. Sharks and whales hunt and eat sea lions. Young sea lions learn to escape. They swim fast and quickly get out of the water.

Pups eat and grow a lot. At about 2 months old, they start to eat fish. They drink milk for at least six months.

Pups learn how to hunt. They eat fish, squid, crabs and octopus. They have sharp teeth for grabbing food. They use their **whiskers** to sense where food is.

Tired sea lions pile together to rest. They **haul** their heavy bodies out of the water onto land or ice. They sometimes gather and float together in the water.

Sea lions are noisy animals. They roar, bark, honk and squeak. They can be heard from many kilometres away. They also make lots of noise underwater!

ALL GROWN UP

Sea lions are fully grown after one year. They live for about 20 to 30 years. Some stay with their family group. Others form new groups.

When sea lions have babies, they return to the beaches where they were born. They have their own babies there.

SEA LIONS AND FISH

Sea lions swim fast to catch fish in the sea. Pretend to be a sea lion with your friends as the fish. How many fish can you catch?

What you need

- an open area for playing
- cones or other items to make boundaries
- a group of players

What you do

1. Use the cones to mark out the "sea". This can be a square or rectangular area.

2. Choose one player to be the sea lion. This person stands in the middle of the "sea".

3. All the other players are fish. Make them stand at one end of the sea.

4. When the sea lion says, "Swim, little fish!", all the fish try to make it to the other side of the sea. If they get caught, they become sea lions. If they make it across, they get to try again.

5. Keep playing until all the fish are caught. Then choose a new sea lion.

Glossary

blubber thick layer of fat under the skin of some animals that keeps them warm

haul pull or drag a weight

mane long, thick hair that grows on the head and neck of some animals

nostril opening in the nose used to breathe and smell

predator animal that hunts other animals for food

prey animal hunted by another animal for food

pup young animal

whisker long, stiff hair growing on the face of some animals

Find out more

Books

Life-size Ocean Animals, Igloo Books (Igloo Books, 2018)

Oceans (DKFindout!), DK (DK Children, 2020)

Sea Lions (Marine Mammals), Ashley Gish (Creative Paperbacks, 2019)

Websites

kids.britannica.com/kids/article/sea-lion/353752
Read more facts about sea lions.

www.dkfindout.com/uk/animals-and-nature/seals-sea-lions-and-walruses/sea-lions/
Learn more about sea lions with DKFindout!

Index

beach 4, 16, 18

blubber 8

diet 4, 6, 14, 15

diving 10

flippers 6, 10

floating 16

fur 8

group 4, 6, 16, 18

habitat 4

hunting 6, 13, 15

ice 4, 16

lifespan 18

mane 8

newborn 4

nostrils 10

predators 13

prey 12

resting 16

sounds 7, 17

speed 12

swimming 10, 12–13

weight 8

whiskers 15